EXPANDED EDITION

SOWERS
Students of the Word

**Digging Deeper
Into
God's Word
Inductively**

By Margie Balcos

Why Dig Deeper?

2nd Timothy 2:15 says, *"Study to show thyself approved unto God, a workman that need not be ashamed, rightly dividing the Word of Truth." (KJV)*

This verse is for all of us, but how do we do this? How do we "rightly divide the Word of Truth"? According to Strong's Concordance and lexicon, to "rightly divide" is **to hold a straight course; doing right; to teach truth directly and correctly.** So, do we just read the Scriptures and meditate on them? That would be good for devotions, but the Scripture clearly says, "Study" and uses the term "workman." In Greek, the word "study" means to exert one's self, to endeavor, to give diligence and the word "workman" means a laborer, someone who labors. We must exert ourselves and labor to hold a straight course, doing right. Then we are to teach truth directly and correctly. In order to accomplish this, we must go beyond just reading the scriptures. We must dig deeper by studying the Scriptures with a new diligence!

Digging deeper into God's Word with SOW'ers is an amazing journey to study the Word of Truth. In this study, you will find and learn to find information to discover the deeper meanings of the Scriptures. You will gain knowledge of the times that will create a fuller picture of the events and help you retain the Scriptures in a new way. Then with this knowledge you will be able to make observations of the Scriptures, interpret them, and then discover how to apply them to your life. This type of study is known as Inductive studying. Some things you will discover and learn to find are:

- God's character and attributes being shown

- Customs of that time

- Maps of the lands mentioned in the book

- Tools and instruments being described in the book

- Information about significant numbers or colors

- Historical Backgrounds of the rulers and land

- Descriptions and facts about the people being talked about

- Key words that have richer meanings in Greek and Hebrew

Studying inductively is not easy and fast. Remember…we are to be diligent laborers. In digging deeper you will see the power of God's Word up close. You will understand what you are reading with more clarity and learn just what the Word is saying to **you** personally! **So, I invite you to come on this incredible Journey! Join me as we become Students Of the Word! (SOW'ers)**

*Remember to download your FREE worksheets! These blank worksheets will enable you to study as many books of the Bible as you want!

See page 59 for detailed instructions on how to download these FREE worksheets.

Dedication

To Danielle, who inspired me to dig deeper into my prayer life and my study in the Word. This deeper prayer and study life truly humbled me. The challenges I encountered, drew me closer to Jesus. This allowed room for Him to use me to bring forth this tool for her and anyone else out there who is ready to dig deeper into their own prayer life and into the Word of God. Danielle's devotion for our study time and the information she was able to learn and retain by studying the Word in this way was encouraging and contagious. Though we faced some tough struggles along the way, we both have seen and experienced the rewards of growing closer to our Savior through studying in His word! Thank you Danielle! You challenged me to dig and really apply what Lord was showing me. I am so grateful for you and the times we shared digging into His Word.

In His Endless Mercy and Love!

Margie Balcos

Acknowledgments

I would like to thank my husband for his tremendous support and understanding of me and my deep desire to study in the Word. His encouragement and love is a special gift that I will always treasure.

I am so grateful for my children who have been so gracious in their understanding of my commitment to see this tool available to everyone and their steadfast prayers for me in this journey.

I would also like to thank Ariel James and Pat Gary, who helped shape SOW'ers through their encouragement, amazing contributions, and relentless prayer support.

 I am so incredibly thankful for the support, prayers and encouragement from LaFon, Grace, Hilary, Pam, David, Justine, Cindy, Debbie, and Johnni. Your gifts of seeing what the Lord has shown me only strengthened my resolve to continue to share this tool with anyone that would listen to me. You all showed me that I am not alone in my journey and I praise the Lord for each and every one of you for allowing the Lord to use you in such a significant way.

How Did We Get Here?

Are you Green and Growing? Are you spiritually growing in the Lord? We all have those valleys in our walk where we become parched and stagnant. Perhaps, we feel we have fallen into complacency. This is not where God would want us to be. The work God has begun in us is not complete. Scripture says, "He who began a good work in you will be faithful to complete it" (Philippians 1:6) He accomplishes this in part through His Word, but we have to study His Word, right?

As a believer in Jesus Christ, we rely on His Word to direct our paths, "Thy Word is a lamp my feet and a light unto my path" (Psalm 119:105). How much of the Word do you understand? Do you know how to apply it to your life? I truly believe that God's Word was written to each of us. I believe that the Holy Spirit can help us understand what the Word is saying and that it is the living Word. "Living" to me means that it grows with me as my understanding of the Scripture grows. If you are a believer, you probably started out learning some verses in Sunday school. Then you gradually grew in your youth group as you began to learn how to apply Scripture to your life and eventually you sat and listened to your pastor(s) share the principles God had revealed to them. Many believers are content to end their growth at this point. I was not, but where was I to begin again? I had a huge burning desire for the Word and an unshakeable need to understand the Scriptures.

I started investing time in small group Bible studies. I saw the benefits of reading the Scriptures for myself and found increasing interest in how differently others in my group interpreted them. I really enjoyed the fellowship and prayer that came with the study.

After a while, those studies became more about filling in the blanks. As a mother of six children, I often would wait until the last possible moment to sit down and do the study. In fact, there were many times, I humbly admit, that I just did not find the time to do the study and did not even attend because I felt so guilty. Then the Lord woke me up to the fact that I was trying to squeeze Him into my life instead of having Him fill and lead my life. For too many years, I used the excuse of a large family and their schedules as my reason and it was time to make a full commitment. I look back and ask myself, "What was I thinking?" and "How did I allow myself to get there?"

I had to break that vicious cycle of putting everything before Jesus. I had to change and by the grace of God, I did. Jesus became my priority and serving Him consumed me. I began leading Bible studies at my church. I enjoyed these studies with new fervor and zeal as the Holy Spirit would guide us in taking the Scriptures and showing us how to apply them in our life. By praying for Jesus to help us apply what we learned in our lives, I began to see God answering the prayers of our group in great ways. Still a hunger for a deeper study continued to grow. What would this study look like?

I have always loved history and archeology. I knew that the knowledge obtained from them along with an understanding of ancient cultures would help me see a better picture of what I was reading. I also strongly believe that God, Jesus, and the Holy Spirit are revealed throughout Scripture. As we study through the Word, we can see the consistency in their character and attributes. Getting to know this helps draw us closer to them and builds an intimate relationship. God is the same yesterday as He is today and will be tomorrow.

Throughout the Bible, we are introduced to many characters. Some characters we can relate to and some are examples for us. Each one has a unique story, yet God is the same and never changing. Watching these characters interact with God and seeing

God's responses to them, gives us great insight to the path God wants us to walk.

Since every word of the Scripture is God-breathed and has a purpose, I needed to understand exactly what I was reading. Over time, we have watered down words so that their true meanings are muddled. In order to understand what I was reading, I needed to understand the words in their intended use. I needed to know the original language and definitions. God does not waste any words. Therefore, careful consideration is needed when reading and words that I did not understand why it was being used or what it meant needed to be investigated.

Having taken a trip to Israel twenty years ago really helped me understand some of the lands during Biblical times. When reading certain passages in Scripture, I could close my eyes and picture the terrain and climate. However, since there are many lands mentioned in the Scriptures I did not get to see, I wanted to be able to picture myself there too. Seeing maps of Biblical times really help us understand some strategic decisions made by certain rulers and by God. Seeing satellite photographs of the lands today almost suffices for being there physically.

Also, having been to other countries around the world, I have had the privilege of experiencing different cultures. When my husband and I travel, we always try to submerge ourselves in the cultures and stay away from tourist hotels and restaurants. We want to see how people live, what they eat, how they dress, and why they believe what they believe. Learning about cultures and customs gives us great insight to a world that we have never known. The Bible is full of different cultures with customs that are sometimes from a world unknown to us. The Bible mentions craftsmen and their designs. These designs are often still used today. They may be tools of the trade or designs of instruments used throughout all levels societies. As I mentioned earlier, I love archeology and seeing how people lived without the comforts of today's modern designs and developments intrigues me greatly.

Another thing that intrigues me is numbers and colors. Seeing in the Scriptures certain numbers being repeatedly used in certain situations was of great interest to me. You can almost sense a foreshadowing of events when certain numbers are being used. The same can be said of colors throughout Scripture. Colors develop a certain symbolism that should be noted. Some of those symbolisms are still recognized today.

Each one of these areas of research was like an ingredient to a meal that would satisfy the hunger I had for understanding the Word. Once these ingredients were obtained, it was time to prepare the "meal". I had to use them all together to understand what I was reading. The full picture was finally coming into focus. I was able to understand the meaning of what I was reading. Then like the most amazing meal ever eaten, I learned what the Word was saying to me. Such a quenching of thirst, such a divine meal it is when we discover how God has lit our path and equipped us with His guidance as we travel on through this journey.

Since I believe that God's Word was written to each of us, I believe it was written to you also. I don't believe that you have to be a scholar, or in seminary to understand what the Scriptures are saying to you. If you are like me and have a hunger for a deeper understanding of the Word, all you have to do is be willing to study. You just need to be willing to put in the effort to discover the ingredients needed to make your "meal".

While looking at some of these "ingredients", I am giving you some questions for you to "chew" or reflect on and pray through. Bon Appetite!

SOWERS
Students of the Word

What Have We Here? Table of Contents

Page   Chapter

11

How Do We SOW?

Though SOW'ers can be used on your own, the benefits of studying with a group will bless you with deep spiritual relationships and will help keep you accountable to completing the study. Therefore, I recommend your first step in SOW'ers to be choosing a group of like-minded friends or family to study with you. It is important to have people that are excited and ready to dig into God's Word. Typically, the only homework is to read the chapter. However, with the expanded version of SOW'ers you will have some extra worksheets that you can choose to do as homework or discuss at the end of your study time. Whichever way you choose to utilize these extra sheets is entirely up to you. The most important thing is to have people that are committed to the group, because you will do all of the studying together. Therefore, try to keep the group to a minimum of three and a maximum of seven.

The second step is to pray over which book to study. If this is your first study in SOW'ers, I would suggest that you choose a smaller book. For example, use Haggai or Jude instead of Genesis or Romans. This would enable you to get accustomed to the flow of the study style. It is very important **to not read** any commentaries or notes, whether in your Bible or on your book shelf. This study is for you to see what God wants to reveal to **you**, not what He has revealed to someone else. At the end of the study, you will have an opportunity to compare your insights with commentaries, but for now, put post-it notes over the commentaries and/or notes in your Bible. I would also encourage you to use various translations of the Bible, as this will help you see some key words very quickly.

Third, gather all your worksheets and resources that you will use during the study. Set up your notebook with the blank worksheets that you have printed from the **free** downloads included with this book. For detailed instructions on how to download these **free** worksheets, see page 59 of this book. Now gather your resources. Remember, your best resource is the Bible, so you will be doing a lot of cross- referencing (looking up correlating verses). Be sure to have a concordance and lexicon available. I recommend <u>Strong's Exhaustive Concordance</u>, which can be found in most bookstores and because it contains a lexicon. Look for books with maps of Biblical lands and Biblical customs and manners. <u>Men of the Bible</u> and <u>Women of the Bible</u> are also excellent resources for mini biographies. You may even want to pick up a time and genealogy chart. Have the internet available as there are many free websites that will be helpful. See the list of suggested resources for more ideas. Remember, **NO COMMENTARIES** at this time.

Finally, set a time for your study. Stick to the time you set. Start on time and be sure to end on time. I suggest you plan for two hours. Use one and a half hours for study and half an hour for prayer time. Again, stick to the designated time for the study out of respect for the others in your group.

Always begin your study with prayer. Start with reading the day's Scripture. Remember that you will end your study time with personal prayer, so the opening prayer is a time to prepare our hearts, minds, eyes, and ears to receive from the Holy Spirit, His Word.

Now you are ready to SOW! Let's get digging!

How Do I Use That?
Resource Help

In order to understand the importance of some of the resource books, you must first understand which books you will need and how to use them. I want to cover a few of the most important resources you will need to get started. Many of these you can find at Amazon.com or your local book store, but some are available on-line for free.

The first is a ***concordance.*** A concordance is a listing of words in alphabetic order that are contained in the text. It gives you all the references of where those words appear in the rest of the book. Seeing how Scripture uses the word in different passages can help us understand the use of the word more clearly. The concordance may also give a brief definition of the root meaning of the word. However, it will not always apply within the context of which the word is being used. Therefore, we cannot rely on the concordance only when doing our study. A concordance is sometimes found in the back of your Bible. Typically, those concordances are limited. Having a separate concordance book gives you a better chance at finding the words you are studying. There are many translations of Scripture. Therefore, try to find a concordance that goes with your translation. Using unrelated translations could hinder your ability to find words. There are many websites that offer different concordance translations that you can access on-line. They are faster to use and easier to navigate. Review suggestions listed on the *"**Where did You Find That?**"* page.

The second important resource book you will need is a ***lexicon***. A lexicon is basically a dictionary of words in their original language. In our case, the languages are Greek and Hebrew. The information you will find in a lexicon are the transliteration of the word and its correct pronunciation, the root word, the part of speech, and an outline of how it is used in the Bible. When looking at this outline, it is crucial that you remember the Old Testament was written in Hebrew and the New Testament in Greek. Scan through the outline carefully to find the exact

Scripture reference you are studying. In this way, you will keep the definition in context intended. Sometimes, a word we use every day will have a much more profound use in the Bible. You will discover this by using the lexicon, which makes it a great tool to have in with your resources.

Often, you will be asked to **_cross-reference_** the Scripture. This is also great tool to use because you are actually using the Bible to research the Bible. Different from using a concordance, cross-referencing takes you on a trip through the Bible to see connections and to fill in the background of what you are reading. You may know that Luke's account of the birth of Jesus is not exactly the same as what you read in the book of Matthew. Not that it is contradictory, but that it contains details that Mathew does not. Reading both, gives us a fuller picture and when you cross-reference those Scriptures with the Old Testament prophecies, you have an even more vivid understanding of what is happening. You can often find cross-references already done for you in your Bible's margins. If not, try using the Treasury of Scripture Knowledge to find them. This is a great help to find those verses you need to complete the picture.

Finally, I would recommend a good book on **_manners, customs or traditions of the Bible._** It is so helpful and exciting to be able to understand symbolisms and rituals when reading the Bible. For instance, understanding the different feasts in the Bible will enhance your comprehension of the climate of the culture. Knowing why certain rituals are performed can explain the mindset of the person you are reading about. Any custom that you can understand can help you in your observations and interpretations of the Scripture.

Of course, there are many more resources you can gather for this study. If you have at least the few listed, you will be on your way to digging into the Scriptures, but be careful to research the authors of the books you choose. You want to be sure that they are not putting their own theology into the books that you are merely using for facts. Look over the suggested resource list to get more ideas of different books to use. Now you are ready!

Where Did You Find That?
Suggested Resources

Remember, in order to do your research, you must first compile your resources. You will first and foremost use the Bible. The Bible never contradicts itself. Therefore cross-referencing will be vital source of information as you explore the Scriptures. You will want to also use a concordance and a lexicon. When using a concordance, remember to use one that goes with your translation of the Scriptures. Having a good atlas and book on customs and traditions are also key to your research. There are many helpful websites that can save you a lot of time and provide many books online for free. If using a phone with internet or iPad, there are many free apps available too. The following are suggestions to get you started. Many of these books can be found on-line for free. **Wikipedia** can be edited by anyone and anonymously, therefore it is **not a reliable** resource and **should NOT be used**.

The Treasury of Scripture Knowledge	*Barbour*
ESV or Strong's Concordance	
Unger's Bible Dictionary	*Merrill Unger*
Nelson's Bible Dictionary	*R. Youngblood, F.F. Bruce, & R.K. Harrison*
Wilson's Old Testament Word Studies	*William Wilson*
All the Men of the Bible	*Lockyer*
All the Women of the Bible	*M. L. del Mastro*
Everyday Biblical Literacy	*J. Stephen Lang*
Where to Find it in the Bible	*Ken Anderson*
Manners and Customs of Bible Lands	*Fred Wright*
Baker's Handbook of Bible Lists	*Andrew E. Hill*
The Seven Festivals of the Messiah	*Edward Chumney*
Foxe's Book of Martyrs	*John Foxe*
Moody Atlas	*Barry J. Beitzel*
Then and Now Bible Maps	*Rose Publishing*
On-Line Resources	
Blueletterbible.com	Biblestudytools.com
e-sword.net	Gotanswers.org
Biblelight.org	Biblestudy.org
Biblegateway.com	ridingthebeast.com
Christiananswers.net	
Studylight.org	
Bible-History.com	

What Have We Done?
Old and New Testament Books

Now that you have your resources, it is time to decide which book of the Bible to study. Use the following lists to help you to decide and keep track of the books you choose. You may want to start with a small book. In an effort to help aide you in your decision, the lists have the number of chapters listed. However, even if a book has a small amount of chapters, those chapters could be very long. So, always preview the book and remember to pray and ask the Holy Spirit to guide you in your choice. Then write your start date and begin. When you have completed your study, you can write in the date you finished and move on to the next study. This study can be used for any and all books of the Bible. Depending on how deep you dig will determine how long the study will take. The only strong advice that can be given is to be consistent with your study and finish well.

What Have We Done?
Old Testament Books

START DATE	END DATE	BOOK	# OF CHAPTERS
		GENESIS	50
		EXODUS	40
		LEVITICUS	27
		NUMBERS	36
		DEUTERONOMY	34
		JOSHUA	24
		JUDGES	21
		RUTH	4
		1 SAMUEL	31
		2 SAMUEL	24
		1 KINGS	22
		2 KINGS	25
		1 CHRONICLES	29
		2 CHRONICLES	36
		EZRA	10
		NEHEMIAH	13
		ESTHER	10
		JOB	47
		PSALMS	150
		PROVERBS	31
		ECCLESIASTES	12
		SONG OF SOLOMON	8
		ISAIAH	66
		JEREMIAH	52
		LAMENTATIONS	5
		EZEKIEL	48
		DANIEL	12
		HOSEA	14
		JOEL	3
		AMOS	9
		OBADIAH	1
January 7,2010	May 20, 2010	JONAH	4
		MICAH	7
		NAHUM	3
		HABAKKUK	3
		ZEPHANIAH	3
		HAGGAI	2
		ZECHARIAH	14
August 10, 2012		MALACHI	4

What Have We Done?

New Testament

START DATE	END DATE	BOOK	# OF CHAPTERS
		MATTHEW	28
		MARK	16
		LUKE	24
		JOHN	21
		ACTS	28
		ROMANS	16
		1 CORINTHIANS	16
		2 CORINTHIANS	13
		GALATIANS	6
		EPHESIANS	6
		PHILIPPIANS	4
		COLOSSIANS	4
September 2011		1 THESSOLONIANS	5
		2 THESSOLONIANS	3
		1 TIMOTHY	6
		2 TIMOTHY	4
		TITUS	3
		PHILEMON	1
		HEBREWS	13
		JAMES	5
		1 PETER	5
		2 PETER	3
		1 JOHN	5
		2 JOHN	1
		3 JOHN	1
		JUDE	1
		REVELATION	22

What Are We Reading?

The first page of our study is basic. Most Bibles contain a lot of this information in the book's introductory page. Remember, when using your Bible try not to look at anything that resembles a commentary. Usually the first couple of verses of the Scripture will reveal a lot of this information, but if not, try cross-referencing the Scriptures to find it. If you use any other resources, be sure to record the resources you used. Sometimes, you will not be able to find the information or you may find it later during your study. Therefore you may have some empty spaces that you will come back to, and in some cases those spaces will remain empty.

__Example:__ "In the second year of King Darius, on the first day of the sixth month, the Word of the Lord came through the prophet Haggai to Zerubbabel son of Shealtiel governor of Judah, and to Joshua son of Jozadak, the high priest." Haggai 1:1 (NKJV)

Date Started 5/2/2011 Date Finished	What Are We Reading?	Resource(s)
Book	*Haggai*	
Author	*Haggai*	
Translation of Bible used	*New King James Version*	
Estimate Date of Writings	*August 29th 520 B.C.* *The 1st day of the sixth month in the second year of King Darius*	*Haggai 1*
To Whom is it Written?	*Zerubbabel and Joshua*	*Haggai 1:1*
From Where is it Written?	*Written, possibly, in Jerusalem, as there is a call to build the house of the Lord, which was left in ruins.*	*Haggai 1:3*
Literary Style	*Exhortation and prophecy*	

How's Your Heart?
Head Knowledge to Heart Change

Every time you open the Bible, you are seeking God. You are trying to discover who He is and what He is saying to you. His Word is alive today and learning how to apply it in your life is essential for your spiritual growth. There is head knowledge, but then there is a heart change required with that new understanding.

In this version of SOW'ers, you will find additional worksheets that will help guide you in this journey. You will be asked questions that are meant to encourage you to look at your heart and really seek those areas that need addressing. Attitudes and actions are changed as we apply the truths found in Scripture. Since the Bible is God-breathed and given to us as a guide to righteous living, we are to study it and learn to use it in our lives. It is crucial for us to take a look at how we are living and compare it to how God wants us to live. As we expose those areas in our lives that need change through our study, we need to prayerfully change in our heart.

The following is an example of the new worksheets that will hopefully help you grow in knowledge and spark a heart change. They will be included with the **free** downloads from the website. These worksheets are intended to correlate with each of the SOW'ers worksheets. However, you may choose to use them all at the same time once you finish your first study. Either way you choose please use these worksheets to look into your heart and discover where there may need to be a change. If you have the knowledge in your mind and can apply it to change in your heart, you will begin to show a greater reflection of Jesus to those around you. Always pray before your begin and consider the questions carefully. Remember to take time to really check your heart.

How's Your Heart?
Head Knowledge to Heart Change

Example: *Complete with, "Who is God? Jesus? And the Holy Spirit?"*
Worksheet

Knowing who God is, does not necessarily mean you know God. Most people when asked will say they know God. However, when pressed for details of who He is...they stumble to think of those attributes or characteristics that truly describe Him. You may know who the President is, but you really do not know him personally. You get to know people by seeing what they say, how they react, and what they do. The more time you spend finding out about someone, the closer you feel towards them. Knowing God's character draws you closer into a relationship with Him. He becomes more personable to you. In this worksheet you will be learning about the character and attributes of the not only of God, but of Jesus and the Holy Spirit, the Trinity. We have many names for God, Jesus and the Holy Spirit, but we want to see their character. First, in Genesis 15:1, God describes Himself as a shield, then in Matthew 28:20 Jesus says He is always with us, and finally in John 19:16 Jesus calls the Holy Spirit "The Helper". All of these descriptions, left on their own are descriptive. However, if we look closer, we can actually see attributes which we can relate to. We realize that as a "shield", God will protect us from our enemies. Also, as Jesus is always with us, He is with us in our times of joy, trials, and despair. We are never alone. Finally, the Holy Spirit as our helper has a big job of both encouraging us as well as guiding us through this journey we call life. Time to Ponder and Pray:

What do you know personally about God? Jesus? The Holy Spirit?

What characteristics and attributes of the Trinity help you to see God, Jesus and The Holy Spirit in a personal way?

Jesus came in the flesh to live as a man, giving us the perfect example of how to live. Getting to know Jesus' characteristics and attributes (what He says, what He does, how He reacts) shows us the model of who we are to strive to be and who we should mirror to others.

Take a look at your own character and attributes, how is your reflection?

Which characteristic or attribute of Jesus do you reflect the most and which ones do you need the Holy Spirit's help with?

What Is Going on Here?
Historical Background

When beginning a study in SOW'ers, it is important to try to get a feel for the climate of the culture. You do this by looking at the political make-up of the society and the spiritual life of the people. You learn who is ruling the people both politically and spiritually. You discover how those people viewed God at this time and what God says about those people and their future. First, read the passage and note any information that you can glean from it. Then try cross-referencing to gain a fuller picture of the scene. This may help in giving a fuller picture of what is going on at the time. Using books like, All the Kings of the Bible or All the Prophecies of the Bible are great resources. Please remember to cross-reference any information you find outside of Scripture to insure the information is accurate. Take a look at the following example to see how to use this page.

Example: (1) "In the second year of **Darius the king**, on the first day of the sixth month, the Word of the Lord came by the **prophet Haggai** to Zerubbabel the son of Shealtiel, governor of Judah, and to **Joshua the son of Jehozadak, the high priest** saying: (2) "Thus says the Lord of hosts, 'This people says, The time has not come, even the time for the house of the Lord to be rebuilt.'"" Haggai 1:1-2 (NKJV)

Time to Dig	What is Going on Here? Historical Background	Resource(s)
What do we know about the ruler(s) of this time?	King Darius was the king of Persia and reigned for 37 years. His name means "lord" son of Hystaspes, 5th from Achaemens, who founded the Persian dynasty. Darius, with the help of 6 Persian chiefs, took the throne from Smerdis Aartxerxes who stole the throne claiming to be the son of Cyrus. Smerdis had destroyed the temples & sent out an edict that forbade the Jews from worshipping. Darius voided that edict and respected the God of the Jews. He died in 455BC	All the Kings of the Bible Studylight.org Ezra 4:7-24
What is the relationship between God and the people at this time?	The people were not making God their priority. He is exhorting them to "think carefully" in this regard. He encourages them with His promises to bring glory to His house.	Haggai Chapters 1&2
Who are the spiritual leaders or prophets of this time? And what are their beliefs?	Haggai name means "festive" 1st to prophecy after captivity. Haggai relied on the Word of the Lord and implored the people to rebuild the temple, which they did. Not much is known about him as we do not know his father's name. Jehozadak is the high priest.	Strong's Concordance H-2292 Cf-Ezra 5:1
Are there any prophecies about the land or people of this place and/or time?	When the people build the temple, God will bless them	Haggai 2:18-19

Who Are God, Jesus, and The Holy Spirit?

Attributes & Characteristics Displayed

Believers know that every part of Scripture is breathed from God. Sometimes you can read the Scriptures so quickly that you fail to see Him and His character. God has breathed and inspired each and every Word. Jesus and the Holy Spirit are acknowledged and active in the Old Testament. You just need to take a closer look at His Word to see each member of the Trinity. You need to dig deeper. Now take a look at each verse and look for the attributes and characteristics of God, Jesus, or the Holy Spirit. Even if His name is not mentioned, His character is displayed through events, people, things, and customs. Therefore, utilize your research to help you with this page. Please take your time with this page, as this is really where you get to discover our Savior. You will get to know Him on a deeper level. You will see how He loves you, His plan for you, and His unwavering grace and mercy for you. You will begin to fully understand how deeply Jesus loves you and how the Holy Spirit is your helper. You are going to be amazed at how their character and attributes are woven throughout Scripture.

Example: *(1)"Paul, a **servant of God** and an **apostle of Jesus** Christ to further the faith of **God's elect** and their knowledge **of the truth** that leads to godliness (2)in the **hope of eternal life,** which **God, who does not lie,** promised **before the beginning of time,** (3)and which now at **His appointed season He has brought to light** through the preaching entrusted to me by the **command of God our Savior,** to Titus, my true son in our common faith: **Grace and peace from God the Father** and **Christ Jesus our Savior.**" Titus 1:1-3 (NIV)*

Verse(s)	**Who Are God, Jesus, and The Holy Spirit?** **Attributes & Characteristics** **Displayed**
1	*God is master, God chooses us*
	God holds truth, Jesus has followers
2	*God does not lie, God promises eternal life*
	God is before time
3	*God controls the time and seasons, God shows us His Word*
	God is commander, God is our Savior
4	*God gives grace and peace, God is the Father*
	Christ Jesus is our Savior

Who Are These People?

People Mentioned in the Text

Continuing to dig deeper you will want to know about the people you are reading about. This page will help you find out their background. Sometimes, there will **not** be a lot of information on a particular person or people readily available. That's okay, keep on digging. Start by reading your cross-references and then try using a concordance or lexicon. There you will find out their name in the original language and what their name means. This can be very telling as to their character or it can be very prophetic. There are many books about people of the Bible you can use or try using the websites recommended on the *"Where Did You Find That?"* page. You can choose to do an extensive biography on each person, or may decide to only obtain information on this person up to the point of which the writing takes place. However you decide to utilize this page is entirely up to you and/or your group.

Example: (1)"**Paul,** an apostle of Christ Jesus by the will of God, and **Timothy** our brother, (2) to the saints and the faithful **brothers and sisters in Christ at Colossae:** Grace and peace to you from God our Father."

Colossians 1:1-2 (ESV)

Character	Who Are These People? People Mentioned in the Text	Resource(s)
Paul (vs. 1) name = "small or little" Strong's Concordance G3972	Born Saul in Taurus Cilicia a Roman Citizen, Jewish, from the tribe of Benjamin, Father was a Pharisee and Paul was a Pharisee Studied under Gamaliel. Persecuted Christians relentlessly until his conversion on the road to Damascus. Passionately and fearlessly preached the Gospel. Baptized by Anias. Established many churches and wrote 14 letters in the Bible. Martyred by decapitation in Rome under Nero's rule 67-68AD	Acts 22:28 Philippians 3:5 Acts 23:6 Acts 22:3 & 34 Acts 9 All the Men of the Bible
Timothy (vs. 1) name= "honouring God" Strong's Concordance G5095	Born in Lystra to Eunice who was Jewish & father was Greek. Brought up to know the Scriptures by mother and grandmother. Faithful in the Lord. Asst. & accompanied Paul in his ministry. 2 letters written to him. Paul made him bishop of the church in Ephesus. It is thought that he interrupted a procession of pagan worshippers to preach the gospel and was dragged & stoned to death in 80AD	Acts 16:1 2Tim. 3:15 1Cr 4:17 1Thess 3:2 1Tim & 2Tim StudyBible.org
The People of Colossae (vs.2) name= "monstrosities" Srong's G2857	A leading city in Asia Minor (modern day Turkey) Faithful brothers and sisters in Christ. Heresy or legalism in regard to Jewish law entered into the church & Paul was contacted to clear the matter up.	Col. 2 Unger's Bible dictionary

What Does That Mean?
Key Words

Key Words can be defined as words or phrases that are essential to the text. They can be nouns, adjectives, or adverbs and if taken out, they leave the passage empty of any meaning. These words are often repeated throughout the text, chapter and book. Usually, they are used to relay an important point. Other times they can give you a deeper understanding of the passage.

In the SOW'ers study, Key Words can also be words that stop you in your reading and cause you to wonder why it was used. They may even be new words to you or are found to be changed in different translations of the Scriptures.

You will be looking these words up in a Bible dictionary, concordance and a lexicon. First, you want to try to look up the words in a concordance that matches the translation you are using. There are lots of computer programs that will make this task easy and quick. You will want to see and note the different ways that it is used. When looking up words in a lexicon, remember that the Old Testament was written in Hebrew and the New Testament was written in Greek. However, there are times when the word is not found in the lexicon. In that case, use a Bible dictionary.

To review what Key words are, ask yourself these questions:

- If removed, does this word or phrase change the meaning of the text?

- Does the word appear repeatedly in the text, chapter, or book?

- Do you know the meaning of the word?

- Does the word stop you, while reading, to ponder it?

- Is the word translated differently in other versions of the Bible?

As you are reading the passage, you may want to have this worksheet handy. You can jot down the words that immediately strike you as a Key Word or simply highlight the words in your Bible and record them here later. If a word is repeated several times, look each one up in a concordance because it may have a different meaning each time it is used. Sometimes the most familiar word has a totally different meaning than what you may think. You may also find that as you continue on with the rest of the study, you will add more words you might have overlooked.

Remember that in the Old Testament, the words should be looked up in the Hebrew lexicon and the New Testament words should be looked up in the Greek lexicon. You can write the word in its original language and annunciation with the part of speech under the Key Word itself. Be aware that there will be times that the word you are looking for will be grouped as a phrase in the lexicon. Continue to look up the phrase and write down what you found.

If you cannot seem to find the word in your lexicon, check to see if there is a cross-reference that may help you locate the synonym for the word. If you still cannot find the word, then try looking it up in the Bible dictionary. Once you have found the definition, re-read the verse with the definition in place of the Key Word to see if it makes sense. In doing this it may also help you see the verse more clearly. As you continue to use this study, this list will become more extensive and your sense for Key Words will increase.

Our example for this worksheet will be extensive. Hopefully, you will observe all the scenarios listed above. Ready?

Example:

*(1) "Finally then, **brethren**, we request and exhort you in the Lord Jesus, that as you received from us instruction as to how you ought to **walk** and **please** God that you excel still more. (2) For you know what commandments we gave you by the **authority** of the Lord Jesus. (3) For this is the will of God, your **sanctification;** that is, that you **abstain** from sexual immorality (4) that each of you know how to **possess** his own **vessel** in **sanctification** and honor, (5) not in lustful passion, like the **Gentiles** who do not know God; (6) and that no man transgress and defraud his brother in the matter because the Lord is the **avenger** in all these things, just as we also told you before and **solemnly** warned you. (7) For God has not called us for the purpose of impurity, but in **sanctification**. (8) So, he who rejects this is not rejecting man but the God who gives His Holy Spirit to you. (9) Now as to the love of the **brethren,** you have no need for anyone to write to you, for you yourselves are taught by God to love one another; (10) for indeed you do practice*
*It toward all the **brethren** who are in Macedonia. But we urge you, **brethren,** to excel still more, (11) and to make it your **ambition** to lead a quiet life and attend to your own business and work with your hands, just as we commanded you, (12) so that you will behave properly toward **outsiders** and not be in any need. (13) But we do not want you to be uninformed, **brethren,** about those who are **asleep,** so that you will not grieve as do the rest who have no hope. (14) for if we believe that Jesus died and **rose** again, even so God will bring with Him those who have fallen **asleep** in Jesus. (15) for this we say to you by the word of the Lord, that we who are alive and remain until the coming of the Lord, will not precede those who have fallen **asleep.** (16) For the Lord Himself will descend from heaven with a **shout,** with the voice of the **archangel** and with the trumpet of God and the dead in Christ will rise first. (17) Then we who are alive and remain will be **caught up** together with the in the clouds to meet the Lord in the air, and so we shall **always** be with the Lord. (18) Therefore, comfort one another with these words."*

1 Thessalonians 4:1-18(NKJV)

Key Word	Verse	**What Does that Mean?** Greek/Hebrew	Resource(s)
Brethren adelphos (n)	4:1, 9, 10, 13	A fellow believer, united to another by the bond of affection	Strong's Con. Lexicon G-80
Please aresko (v)	4:1	To accommodate one's self to the opinions, desires, and interests of others	Strong's Con. Lexicon G-700
Walk peropateo (v)	4:1	To regulate one's life. Conduct one's self.	Strong's Con. Lexicon G-4043
Holy/Sanctification hagiasmos (n)	4:3 4:4, 7	Opposed to lust in the effect of purification/consecration of heart of life	Strong's Con. Lexicon G-38
Possess ktaomai (v)	4:4	To marry a wife; express completely the idea of marrying in contrast with the baseness of procuring a harlot as his "vessel"	Strong's Con. Lexicon G-2932
Vessel skeuos (n)	4:4	Common metaphor for body is used of a woman, as the vessel of her husband	Strong's Con. Lexicon G-4632
Avenger ekdikos (adj)	4:16	Exacting penalty from one, punisher	Strong's Con. Lexicon G-1558
Study/Aspire philotimeomai (v)	4:11	From a love of honor. To strive to bring something to pass to make it one's aim	Strong's Con. Lexicon G-5389
Archangel archaggelos (n)	4:16	One of the chiefs/leaders of the angels	Strong's Con. Lexicon G-743
Shout keleusma (n)	4:16	A command given with a loud summons	Strong's Con. Lexicon G-2752
Will be caught up harpazo (v)	4:17	Used of divine power transferring a person marvelously and swiftly from one place to another...to snatch	Strong's Con. Lexicon G-726
We shall always pantote (adv)	4:17	At all times...ever	Strong's Con. Lex. G-3842

Where Are We?
Places Mentioned in the Text

On this sheet you will be looking for maps and descriptions of the land or city. You may use the maps in your Bible or use the internet to find and print maps. Descriptions can be found by using a concordance or a lexicon. You can also use the Moody Atlas, but be sure to indicate your resources. Try to find a map of the place in Biblical times as well as where it would be on today's map. Then and Now Bible Maps is a great tool to accomplish this task. However, if you can find the exact latitude and longitude degrees, you may be able to use Google Earth on the internet and see the location today via satellite. This is really an amazing view and you will really get a feel for the terrain and understand distances between lands. It may also help you understand some of the cultures of that time. Try to print a copy of the maps you find and keep them with your study. It is great to highlight those towns and cities mentioned. Determining distances between towns and the terrain can help you visualize the travel time and level of difficulty it would take to travel. Having a copy in your book will help you reflect on them during your study.

Example: (7) "as **Sodom** and **Gomorrah**, and the cities around them in a similar manner to these, having given themselves over to sexual immorality and gone after strange flesh, are set forth as an example, suffering the vengeance of eternal fire." Jude 7 (NKJV)

Verse	Where Are We? Places Mentioned in the Text	Resource(s)
Sodom Jude 7	*Its name is from the Greek word "Sodoma" meaning burning It was a city destroyed by the Lord when he rained down fire and brimstone upon it.* *See Attached Map* *A city caught up in "grave sin" whose outcries had come up to the Lord*	*Strong's Concordance and Lexicon G-4670* *Moody Atlas* *Cross-Ref. Genesis 18:20-19:29*
Gomorrah Jude 7	*Its name is from the Greek word "Gomorra" meaning "submersion." It was a city in the eastern part of Judah which was destroyed by the Lord when He rained down fire and brimstone upon it. It is now believed to be covered by the Dead Sea* *See Attached Map*	*Strong's Concordance and Lexicon G-1116* *Moody Atlas*

What Is That?

Tools & Instruments

Many times in Scripture there are tools and instruments mentioned. Sometimes they are meant to be symbolic and other times they are mentioned to give a fuller picture of the culture. As you do the study, you will be able to tell which way the author is intending for them to be understood. On this worksheet you will do research to find out the physical attributes of the tools or instruments mentioned. You will want to see how they were used in the culture of the times. Therefore, you may want to look them up in one of your customs and traditions of Biblical Times resources. The internet may help provide a beginning step, but remember **<u>do not</u>** use **WIKIPEDIA**. Only use reliable internet resources. Take a look at the ***"Where Did You Find That?"*** page for some suggested websites and book resources. Then, take a look for definitions through a concordance and a lexicon. Try to find pictures of them in a dictionary and if possible, print a copy for you to keep with your study. Believe it or not, some tools and instruments are still used by certain cultures today. If you find this to be true, you may want to include pictures of today's version of the tool or instrument and its current use. If you are a gadget person, this can be really interesting, but remember to keep the tool or instrument in the context of the Scriptures being explored.

Examples: *"Is it a time for you yourselves to dwell in your **paneled houses**, while this house lies in ruins?"* **Haggai 1:4 (NKJV)**

*"...how did you fare? When one came to a heap of twenty measures, there were but ten. When one came to the **wine vat** to draw fifty measures, there were but twenty."* **Haggai 2:16 (NKJV)**

*"On that day, declares the Lord of Hosts, I will take you. O Zerubbabel my servant, the son of Shealtiel, declares the Lord, and make you like a **signet ring**. For I have chosen you, declares the Lord of Hosts."* **Haggai 2:23 (NKJV)**

Verse	What Is That? Tools and Instruments	Resource(s)
1:4 Paneled/ceiled house caphan (n)	These were homes that were covered inside with imported cedar from floor to ceiling. These were homes that surrounded the temple. In Biblical days, they were considered luxurious.	Strong's Con. H5603 CF 1Kings 7:3-7 Jermiahn 22:14-15
2:16 Wine vat/ wine press yeqeb (n)	A shallow pit cut into solid rock, into which grape juice flowed. When grapes were trodden & where it was retained until fermentation had begun. Juice was later transferred to jars or skins for further fermentation and storage.	Bible Dictionary See Attached picture
2:23 Signet ring chowtham(n)	A seal that functions as a signature. In Hebrew times, it was a ring that possibly was carried on a string and worn around the neck.	Strong's Con H2368 See Attached picture

What Are They Doing? And Why are They Doing It?

Customs

Another part of digging is finding out about the customs of that time period. Customs are a crucial part of every society or group of people. Every country has specific customs that can explain a lot about the people, what the people are doing and why they are doing it.

Researching these customs is both interesting and helpful for you to understand the culture of the people in the Scriptures you are reading. Some customs are so important to their people that they are still practiced on today. Their origins can help you understand their significance and help you interpret what you are reading.

Many customs can be traced back through the Old Testament. Therefore, you can start by cross-referencing the Scripture as you come upon them in your reading. Historians have discovered many customs through their research of various tribes. Therefore, you may find that using other resources can add more details. Just be sure that the resource is factual and not opinion driven. Try using Strong's Concordance, Every Day Living in Biblical Times or Logos' Manners and Customs of the Bible to help. However, there are many Biblical websites that offer even more resources about how the custom is practiced today. See the Recommended Resources page for more places to research customs.

Always make sure to cross-check your resources. There will be times that customs are not easily seen. However, over time you will develop an eye for spotting them. Just ask yourself one of these questions, "What are they doing?" or "Why are they doing that?." Then write them down and start your search!

Take a look at the following example to help you see some places where customs are not as obvious.

Example:

*(1) "Meanwhile Boaz went up to the **town gate and sat down** there just as the kinsman had mentioned came along. Boaz said, 'Come over here my friend, and sit down.' So he went over and sat down. (2)Boaz took **ten of the elders** of the town and said, 'Sit here, ' and they did so. (3) Then he said to the kinsman, "Naomi, who has come back from Moab, is **selling the piece of land** that belonged to our relative Elimelech. (4) I thought I should bring the matter to your attention and suggest that you buy it in the presence of these seated here and in the presence of the elders of my people. If you will redeem it, do so. But if you will not, tell me, so I will know. For no one has the right to do it except you, and I am next in line.' 'I will redeem it" he said. (5)Then Boaz said, 'On the day you buy the land from Naomi, you also **acquire Ruth the Moabite, the dead man's widow,** in order to maintain the name of the dead with his property.' (6)At this the kinsman said, 'Then **I cannot redeem** it because I might endanger my own estate. You redeem it yourself. I cannot do it.'(7) Now in earlier times in Israel, for the redemption and transfer of property to become final, **one party took off his sandal** and gave it to the other. This was the method of legalizing transactions in Israel. (8)So the kinsman said to Boaz, 'Buy it yourself.' And he removed his sandal. (9)Then Boaz announced to the elders and all the people, 'Today you are witnesses that I have bought from Naomi all the property of Elimelech, Kilion, and Mahlon.' "*   **Ruth 4:1-9 (NIV)**

Verse	What Are They Doing and Why Are They Doing It? Customs	Resource(s)
1 "sitting at the town gate" "kinsman"	The custom of using gates as places for public deliberation Basically the holding of court where trials were held; citizens gathered for business etc. Redeemer: It was the duty of the kinsman to redeem the paternal estate that his nearest relative might have sold through poverty; If there was no kinsman then the compensation went to the priest representing Jehovah	Unger's Bible Dictionary CR 2Sam 15:2 Strong's Con. H-8179 CR Deu 25:5 CR Lev 25:25
2 "Ten of the elders"	Full court of legal proceedings. They were to see that the laws regarding the death of a brother/kinsman were carried out accordingly.	CR Deu 25:7
3 "selling the piece of land"	It would appear that Elimelech sold his land before he left for Moab. According to the Law at that time, his oldest brother had a right to purchase it back and redeem his brother. If a brother was not able to accomplish this, then it went to the nearest relative.	CR Lev 25:25
5 "you also acquire Ruth the dead man's widow"	Along with redeeming the land, the oldest brother was allowed to marry the widow of his brother. If the widow were to bear a son, that son would then be able to bring back the name of the man that died and carry on his inheritance.	CR Deu 25:5 CR Lev 25:25
6 "I cannot redeem"	If the kinsman marries the widow and she bears a son, that son could receive that kinsman's entire inheritance. Therefore, the kinsman did not want to take the chance.	Ruth 4:6
7 "one party took off his sandal"	A public ritual to pass one's property rights to another, removing his sandal and passing it to the new owner. This is most likely from the fact that the right to tread the soil belonged only to the owner of it, and so the transfer of a sandal was appropriately symbolic of transferring property. It is said that this practice carries on in the East even today.	CR Ps 60:10 CR Gen 14:23 CR Josh 15:5 Logo's Customs & Manners

Why that Number or Color?
Significant Numbers & Colors

Throughout the Scriptures, specific numbers are mentioned. As these numbers appear over and over again, they sometimes build toward a specific meaning. Therefore, when we see these numbers appear it helps us to understand the deeper meaning of the passage. For example, think about the number forty. How long did it rain on the earth while Noah and his family were in the ark? How long was Moses in the desert alone? How long did the Israelites wander in the desert after their escape from Egypt? How many days was Moses on Mount Sinai to receive the Ten Commandments? How many days did Jesus and Elijah fast in the desert? The common number in these examples is the number forty. Each example is one of either testing or trial. When you read Jonah, you will discover that God had given the people of Ninevah only "forty" days before the Lord would pour out His wrath on them and their city and destroy them both. Therefore, you can see that whenever the number forty is used, you need to look at that Scripture in terms of an ensuing test or trial period. In each of these cases, there is either rescue or retribution by God at the end of this period.

Likewise, colors have some significance within Scripture. They help us to visualize the scene and help us to see deeper into the characters and culture of the times. For instance, let's look at the color purple. This color was not easily accessible to everyone during Biblical times. Purple dye was painstakingly retrieved from a special type of shellfish. To possess a robe in this color meant that you were either wealthy or part of royalty. Most of the time you will find this color in Scripture in conjunction with fine linens being worn by someone of wealthy stature, like a king. When Jesus was being taunted by the Roman guards, they placed a thorn of crowns on his head and what color was the robe they draped on Him? What color robe was Daniel clothed in by command of Belshazzar? What color were the ten tabernacle curtains? The answer is purple.

As you are reading, make note of any specific numbers or colors. First, look them up in a concordance and read the other verses that contain that number or color. See if you can determine a pattern of uses.

Always remember to record your resources, but be very careful of the ones that you use. There are many resources on-line to help you with meanings, but some resources can use a non-Scriptural bias and mystify the color or number which can distort them from their intended use.

Believers know that power is not in the color or the number, it is in Jesus Christ! Remember to check the resource page to see some helpful places for you to use in your research.

Example of number:
*"There shall be **twelve** stones with names according to the names of the sons of Israel. They shall be like signets, each engraved with its name, for the **twelve** tribes."* **Exodus 39:14 (KJV)**

Example of color:
*(18)"Behold, when we come into the land, you shall tie this **scarlet** cord in the window through which you let us down, and you shall gather into your house your father, mother, your brothers and all your father's household. (19)Then if anyone goes out of the doors of your house into the street, his blood shall be on his own head, and we shall be guiltless. But if a hand is laid on anyone who is with you in the house, his blood shall be on our head."* **Joshua 2:18-19**

Verse	Why That Number or Color? Significant Numbers & Colors	Resource(s)
14 "twelve" Shenayim (adj/n)	This number appears 161 times in the Bible. It is considered a cardinal number. It can signify governmental perfection. 12 disciples/apostles, Jesus first recorded teaching age was 12 The number twelve was also used in the construction of the temple both on earth and in Heaven. Many altars were constructed using twelve stones.	Strong's Concordance H8147 Biblestudy.org ESV Concordance
18 "scarlet" shanity(n)	Properly, the insect 'coccus ilicis', the dried body of the female that yields coloring matter from which is made the dye used for cloth to color it scarlet or crimson. This color appears 49 times in the Bible. Usually it is associated with the color purple and blue. Exodus 25:4, 26:1,31, &36, 27:16, 28:5,6,15,33 &39:24,29 Usually, it is in the form of a thread, yarn or cloth When not found in the association, it can be seen as a marker of some sort signifying something to take notice of. First born in Genesis 38:28, Bathsheba's lips in Song of Solomon 4:3 Our sins in Isaiah 1:18	Strong's Concordance H8144 ESV Concordance

What Do We Know Now?
Inductive Verse by Verse

Now that you have dug deep into The Word and obtained all of your research, it is time to piece together all the information discovered. Each page has been purposed for this particular exercise. You now get to articulate what you labored for in your study time. You do this by going verse by verse through the Scripture and breaking it down in to three sections.

On this worksheet, you will record your observations, then your interpretations, and finally you will apply what you have learned to your own life. You will want to have all of your research handy and available. Many times, you may find yourself cross-referencing again or looking up missed key words. Make sure you have your Bible, concordance and a lexicon handy and remember to record any new information you gain.

To begin this process, always start with prayer. Then, look at each verse and record your *observations* as you know them. When reading each verse, ask "What am I reading?" or "What is the passage about?" In order to maintain the complete thought of the verse, it may be necessary to group several verses together. This will insure you stay within the context of the Scripture. It is here that you will be able to "fill" in the picture of the Scripture with all of your research. Try not to merely paraphrase the verse(s). Really dig into what information you found and record it here. Sometimes, there will not be much information to record, but do not be discouraged. You will be amazed at what you will see as you continue on.

Once you complete the observation of the verse(s), you will then interpret it. This is where you want to be sure you have spent time in prayer, as this is when the Holy Spirit can open your eyes to see what God is saying. Ask yourself these questions before you begin, "What does it mean?" or "Why does this matter?" Then using your observations of the verse(s), fill in the *interpretation* section with your answers.

43

Remember to keep it in context of what you are reading. Consider each verse or group of verses in light of its surrounding verses. Do not make the mistake of twisting verses to support a meaning that is not clearly being taught. Let the passage speak for itself. Review the historical background and culture of the time. Do not add to what the author is saying. Keep in mind that Scripture never contradicts itself and remember the literary style of the book. There will be times that you will find the interpretation section will be difficult to see quickly, but keep praying and digging, as you wait on the Lord to reveal it to you. This will become easier as you continue through each step.

The last and most important step in this process is *application*. This is the time to look at how to apply the Scriptures to your life. In this section, you will look at the interpretations and see how they relate to you. Remember that the Scriptures were written to and for you! They teach you, correct you and encourage you. They may also expose to you those areas in your thinking and beliefs that do not align with the Word of God and hopefully cause you to repent. (2 Timothy 3:16) Ultimately, they will draw you close to God.

Begin by asking yourself, "What does it mean to me?" "How does this look in my life?" or "What is God trying to teach me?" You may want to fill this space in with a question to yourself. It is in the application that you will tend to see your current spiritual state and your need for growth. Therefore, really think about this area and your answers. Search your relationship with Jesus and your spiritual walk to see how to apply the Scriptures in your own life. Search for how the Gospel is represented in the passage and how to apply it.

My hope is that you will not only see the applications, but you will actually take the steps to apply them to your life. This is good homework for you to consider. I have included two examples for you to review, one in the New Testament and one in the Old Testament. Look closely at the applications as you can see that the Old Testament has applications for all of us today! Remember that the applications are what God is showing **you** and He may show you something different each time you read His Word. Therefore, the following are merely examples of what He has shown me at a specific time in my walk. The most amazing fact about the Word of God is that it never grows old. Every time I read it, it shows me a new area in my life where I need to apply it. Amazing!

Example 1:

(1) "Paul a bond-servant of God and an apostle of Jesus Christ, for the faith of those chosen of God and the knowledge of the truth which is according to godliness, (2)In the hope of eternal life, which God, who cannot lie, promised long ages ago, (3) but at the proper time manifested, even His word, in the proclamation with which I was entrusted according to the commandment of God our Savior, (4) To Titus, my true child in a common faith: Grace and peace from God the Father and Christ Jesus our Savior. (5) For this reason I left you in Crete, that you would set in order what remains and appoint elders in every city as I directed you, (6) namely, if any man is above reproach, the husband of one wife, having children who believe, not accused of dissipation or rebellion. (7) For the overseer must be above reproach as God's steward, not self-willed, not quick-tempered, not addicted to wine, not pugnacious, not fond of sordid gain, (8) but hospitable, loving what is good, sensible, just devout, self-controlled, (9) holding fast the faithful word which is in accordance with the teaching, so that he will be able both to exhort in sound doctrine and to refute those who contradict." **Titus 1:1-9 (NASB)**

What Do We Know Now?
Inductive Verse by Verse

Verse(s)	Observation: What is the passage about?	Interpretation: What does the passage mean?	Application: What does it mean to ME?
1:1	Introduction of Paul as a bondservant, teacher, and apostle	Paul is fervent in teaching the gospel	I need to listen to Paul teachings
1:2-3	God does not lie. He promised hope of eternal life & has shown it to them.	God is trustworthy & has given us hope for eternal life	I need to trust God & thank Him for giving me eternal life
1:4	This letter is to Titus who is a brother in faith. Peace and grace come from Jesus Christ our Lord.	Our faith bonds us to the family of Jesus Christ	Do I seek to bond with fellow believers?
1:5	Paul left Titus in Crete to finish setting up the church	There are guidelines to setting up a church and elders are appointed	Do I respect the church's order?
1:6-9	Attributes of the church's elders	God has very specific attributes for the leadership of the church	Do the leaders of my church reflect these attributes?

Example 2:

(1) "In the days when the judges ruled there was a famine in the land, and a man of Bethlehem in Judah went to sojourn in the country of Moab, he and his wife and his two sons. (2)The name of the man was Elimelech and the name of his wife Naomi, and the names of his two sons were Mahlon and Chilion. They were Ephrathites from Bethlehem in Judah. They went into the country of Moab and remained there. (3)But Elimelech, the husband of Naomi, died, and she was left with her two sons. (4)These took Moabite wives the name of the one was Orpah and the name of the other Ruth. They lived there about ten years, (5) and both Mahlon and Chilion died, so that the woman was left without her two sons and her husband. (6) Then she arose with her daughters-in-law to return from the country of Moab, for she had heard in the fields of Moab that the Lord had visited His people and given them food. (7)So she set out from the place where she was with her two daughters-in-law, and they went on the way to return to the land of Judah. (8)But Naomi said to her two daughters-in-law, 'Go, return each of you to her mother's house. May the Lord deal kindly with you as you have dealt with the dead and with me. (9)The Lord grant that you may find rest, each of you in the house of her husband!' Then she kissed them, and they lifted up their voices and wept. (10)And they said to her, 'No, we will return with you to your people.'" **Ruth 1:1-9 (ESV)**

What Do We Know Now?
Inductive Verse by Verse

Verse(s)	Observation: What is the passage about?	Interpretation: What does the passage mean?	Application: What does it mean to ME?
1:1	*Sometime between 1100-722BC the Lord brought about a famine in Judah. Elimelech fled with his family to Moab.*	*God's people were disobedient and He disciplined them with a famine. Elimelech fled his punishment.*	*What do I do when being punished?*
1:2-3	*The family of Elimelech is from Bethlehem from the tribe of Ephrathites and they fled 60miles to pagan land of Moab where Elimelech died.*	*Elimelech and his family are part of God's people and ran from God to Moab, Israel's enemy. God allowed Elimelech to die.*	*Don't run from God or His punishment. Do I run to God or away from Him when I sin?*
1:4-5	*Mahlon & Chilion married Moabite women, Orpah & Ruth. 10 years later these brothers died leaving no heirs.*	*Mahlon & Chilion married idol worshippers Unrepentant, God allowed them to die without children.*	*How do handle my consequences to my sin?*
1:6-7	*Word spread that the famine was over. Naomi set out to head back to Judah with her daughters-in-law.*	*God forgave the Israelites and removed the famine. Naomi wants to return to Judah.*	*God forgives when I repent. When I repent do I feel I can go "home"?*
1:8-10	*Naomi releases her daughters-in-law to return home to their families. They did not want to depart from her.*	*Naomi gave her daughters-in-law a choice to go back to their pagan lives. Ruth chose to stay with her.*	*When given the choice, do I choose a life with God or idols?*

What Do I Think?
My Thoughts and Commentary

Once you have taken all the facts, made your observations, interpreted those observations and discovered their applications in your life, you are ready to record your thoughts on the book. This is a free space for you to write all those insights that the Holy Spirit has revealed to you. You may want to have your notebook open to review your research.

There are a few different ways to utilize this page. You may want to go verse by verse and explain how you came to your interpretations and applications or you may want to summarize the life lessons and interesting facts that you discovered throughout the study in the book.

Which way you choose to do this page is up to you. **There is no right or wrong way**. In fact, you may find that your thoughts on how to do this page will change depending on the book you study. It is very important that you complete this page. This is the place for you to summarize all the research you have done. If you are meeting in a group, I want to encourage you to do this page during your study time, as it will help hold you accountable to finish. You will feel the blessing of completion as you finish this worksheet.

Please do not be intimidated by this crucial step. This is for **you** to organize your thoughts and is for your eyes only, unless you choose to share it.

Read the two examples to help you understand just some of the different ways to utilize this worksheet.

What Do I Think?
My Thoughts/Commentary

Example 1:

Jude

In 65AD Jesus' brother Jude (name means "praise") writes this letter not only to believers of this time, but to all of us even today. This letter is relevant to you and me today! Without haste, Jude shares his concern about ungodly men that are sneaking into the churches. Jude warns us to beware and fight for our faith. In Galatians, Paul tells us "...but it was because of the false brethren secretly brought in, who had snuck in to spy out our liberty which we have in Christ Jesus, in order to bring us into bondage." These men were seeking nothing but destruction of the Gospel and those that chose to believe. Many times we read these men have "crept in" or "slipped in" secretly. These men are masters at what they do and looking in Strong's G3924 it says they "steal in or slip in stealthily." You may not notice them as they are in "stealth" mode. Even more so should we be on the watch for them. These men exist only to condemn us. These "posers" of Christians can be identified by their empty works and the destruction it leaves behind. Jude reminds us of what happened in Egypt with these men, which shows us that they existed then, now, and will continue to exist until the "End of Days" or "Judgment Day." These men are wicked to the core. This corruption did not merely exist with men but in verse 6 we learn that it existed even with some of the angels. But just as God judged these men, He did even more so with the angels. Whole cities like Sodom and Gomorrah were not able to escape His judgment. One of our duties as believers is to be aware of these wicked men and watch for them. Now what do we do when confronted with these ungodly men? The archangel Michael shows us. As Jude recalls Michael's response to Satan during the dispute over the body of Moses, he demonstrates that it is not in our own strength, but we are to call upon the Lord. We are to cast them out, in Jesus' name, to be rebuked by the Lord. Jude ends his letter by imploring believers to continue to build

their faith through prayer and obedience all the days of our lives.
We are to hate the sin, but reach the sinner in love. Remember, it
is Jesus that keeps us from stumbling and purifies us in the Day of
Judgment. It is His gracious sacrifice that makes it possible for all
of us to have victory over death and the evil one. Amen!

What Do I Think?
My Thoughts/Commentary

Example 2:

Colossians

(Chapter 1)
Paul writes this letter to not only the people of Colossae, but to
"faithful brothers and sisters in Christ." Epaphras, a Jewish
Christian, has been sharing the gospel with the Colossians
faithfully and would report to Paul of their great faith and love.
Paul understands that their faith will be tested and therefore prays
for them continuously. What Paul does not pray for is safety. He
prays for them to have growing knowledge, patience, endurance,
and strength. This is spiritual growth. Their physical body is
under protection of God. What Christ did on the cross was and is
sufficient for us, for we are saved through Christ.

Paul is, once again, explaining just who Christ is. Paul lists many
attributes of God. He is the creator, is invisible, forgiving,
rescuer, deliverer, grace, patient, mighty, powerful, giver of
knowledge, and the Father. Jesus' sacrifice is perfect. Paul goes
on to show how being a believer we are changed in our behavior
and attitudes. He illustrates how we are only holy through Christ.
Paul exhorts us to be firm...to not move from the hope.

Paul gave up everything-power, position, money, and friends to be
a servant for Christ. Even in chains, Paul rejoices! He rejoices
with being called by Christ and being given the "mystery" of all
the ages. He has a great work ahead of him yet. Also, this mystery

is being made known to the gentiles. Only with wisdom are they able to teach and admonish. Paul's goal is for all believers to take steps towards maturity-not away from it. Because of this goal, he constantly battles the attacks of the enemy.

(Chapter2)

Paul's love for the brothers and sisters is great as he continues to pray and battle spiritually for them. He longs for them to be encouraged. Though he cannot be with them physically, he lets them know he is with them spiritually and that they fill his thoughts, his heart, and his prayers.

Paul warns them to stand firm on their knowledge and not to be swayed by persuasive talk. There are those which seek to deceive them. We remember that Christ is ruler over us when we believe and accept His grace, we submit to His authority. Because Christ dwells in us, we have been changed and therefore circumcised spiritually from the world. We are made new and once we were dead, we are now alive. Through His resurrection, we are raised with Him and made alive spiritually. The things of this world that try to pull us away from Christ, He has overcome and given us victory over. Our debt is paid in full by Jesus' precious blood that He shed on the cross.

(Chapter 3)

Now that we are rendered debt free, we must not continue to accrue debt. We are called to live in our freedom and lead by example. Paul begins now to instruct us in how we are to live as believers. He encourages us to put away our old self and provoke God's consequences. Sometimes you never know when those consequences will come, but they will come. We must make conscious efforts to turn away from sin. No excuses. We know what sin is and that there are consequences. We are all on the same level as sinners and believers. Specifically, Paul calls us out on harboring anger, wrath, malice, slander, abusive speech and disobedience. We are to be the opposite. We are to have a heart of compassion, kindness, humility, gentleness, patience, and forgiving of one another. We are to be unified.

Specifically, Paul dives into behaviors of family. Wives are to submit to their husbands. Not in slavery, but in obedience to the Lord. This is how the Lord wants it. In turn, Paul not only instructs the husbands to love their wives, but to not treat them harshly. Submission is a form of respect and if a wife respects her husband he has nothing to embitter his heart against her. Children are to obey both parents. This pleases the Lord. In turn, parents are to not to provoke their children. This cycle is set for a role model of the family as the Lord wants it and it is good.

(Chapter 4)
Love is the greatest virtue and is the bond for us as believers. Paul continues with sending us into the workforce and how we are to represent the Lord. Servants are to obey their masters at all times, meaning employees are to obey their employers. It is the nature of our world to have a "boss." It is important that we reflect Christ in every aspect of our lives. This includes the workplace. If we do what is right in the Lord, He will protect us. If we reflect Him in the workplace, how much more will we see Him working in us. We serve others because we serve the Lord, who served others and more importantly, served God. But Paul is not finished, now he mentions the masters or employers to us. They are to be fair and just, knowing that they themselves have a master greater than they, Jesus!

Paul exhorts them and us to be devoted in prayer and have thankful hearts. He reminds us to pray for those serving the Lord and to walk in wisdom. Our speech should always be uplifting and gracious, but also we are to be mindful of how we answer to those seeking the gift of the gospel. We should take the gift of our position seriously and use it for Christ.

Paul closes his letter exhorting each of us to be open about our lives with each other and to remember those co-laborers in Christ. We are to do what we can to encourage them and help them as we should with each other. Paul is not alone in this ministry and reminds them who the other co-laborers are and their need of prayer and encouragement. Paul wants all believers to receive these instructions.

What Did They Say?
The Commentators

The last step in SOW'ers is to finally look at what the commentators said. You can finally take off those Post-its that you used to cover the notes and comments in your Bible. Now you have an opportunity to see what studied Biblical scholars and theologians have found and what God has spoken to them. Remember, that God speaks to all of us in His Word. What He speaks and reveals to you may be slightly different than what He has spoken and shown to others. Therefore, reading other commentaries should only help you gain another perspective that adds to the overall message from God.

The following worksheet is to record those insights. Everyone is at different stages of maturity in their spiritual walk and as they grow in their maturity the Word will reveal more to them. That is part of why His Word is called "the Living Word". Therefore, do not be discouraged if you feel that you missed something that other commentators grasped.

Simply list the verses you are comparing and make note of any differences or specific interesting remarks made by the commentator. I suggest using at least three commentators. Some recommended commentators are Matthew Henry, Vernon J. McGee, Chuck Smith, Charles Stanely, Kay Arther, R. C. Sproul, David Guzik, Jon Courson, Charles Spurgeon and Karen Jobes. Most of these you can obtain for **free** on the internet through various websites and sometimes through blueletterBible.com.

Example:

"Jude, a servant of Jesus Christ and brother of James. To those who are called, beloved in God the Father and kept for Jesus Christ:"   ***Jude 1(ESV)***

"(3) Beloved, although I was very eager to write to you about our common salvation, I found it necessary to write appealing to you to contend for the faith that was once for all delivered to the saints. (4) For certain people have crept in unnoticed who long ago were designated for this condemnation, ungodly people, who pervert the grace of our God into sensuality and deny our only Master and Lord, Jesus Christ. Now I want to remind you, although you once fully knew it, that Jesus, who saved a people out of the land of Egypt, afterward destroyed those who did not believe. (6) And the angels who did not stay within their own position of authority, but left their proper dwelling, he has kept in eternal chains under gloomy darkness until the judgment of the great day—(7) just as Sodom and Gomorrah and the surrounding cities, which likewise indulged in sexual immorality and pursued unnatural desire, serve as an example by undergoing a punishment of eternal fire. (8) Yet in like manner these people also, relying on their dreams, defile the flesh, reject authority, and blaspheme the glorious ones. (9) But when the archangel Michael, contending with the devil, was disputing about the body of Moses, he did not presume to pronounce a blasphemous judgment, but said, "The Lord rebuke you." (10) But these people blaspheme all that they do not understand, and they are destroyed by all that they, like unreasoning animals, understand instinctively.(11) Woe to them! For they walked in the way of Cain and abandoned themselves for the sake of gain to Balaam's error and perished in Korah's rebellion. (12) These are hidden reefs at your love feasts, as they feast with you without fear, shepherds feeding themselves; waterless clouds, swept along by winds; fruitless trees in late autumn, twice dead, uprooted; (13) wild waves of the sea, casting up the foam of their own shame; wandering stars, for whom the gloom of utter darkness has been reserved forever"
Jude 1:4-13 (ESV)

Verse(s)	**What Did They Say?** **The Commentators**	Resource(s)
1	*"Even though Jude was Jesus' half-brother*, He only identifies himself as a bond servant. This fact shows his humility and reminds us that the connection to Jesus is as relative as being an actual relative. Jude valued the fact that Jesus was his half-brother, but understood the greater connection of Jesus being his Lord and Savior."*	**Mark 6:3 & Matthew 13:55 David Guzik*
3-16	*"Jude was intending to write about salvation and the Holy Spirit had him change his epistle to cover the concerns over the apostasy using graphic details to get the point across."*	*Veron J. McGee*

Prayer & Praise
Time for Personal Growth

Prayer is an essential part of SOW'ers. This page should be done at each study time. Always allow yourself plenty of time for this important step. Everyone should agree that all praises and prayers are to stay in the group and not to be shared with anyone else. Everyone needs to have trust in this principle in order to really open up and become real with each other. This is a time of intimacy within the group and should be respected.

Many times in prayer, you may end up asking for help in everything and forgetting to thank the Lord for all He has done. Like a child to a parent, "I want You to...," "I need You to...," "Please give me..." Amen. Therefore, you will first offer one praise report. It always amazes me that some struggle with this essential part of prayer. All you need to ask yourself is, "What has the Lord done for me today?" This could be as simple as allowing you to be at the study or as intimate as showing His provision and love for you in a special way. Our Lord is so gracious and His blessings are plenty. Thank Him for them. Let Him know that you recognize His desire and will to supply all your needs right down to a good night's sleep.

Next, think about what the Lord has shown you through His Word today and how you might apply it to your life. Make this prayer about **you!** There are other venues for prayers for family and friends. Also, this is not a time to gossip about others. Please be cautious of what you say. This is a time for you to get personal and begin to dig deeper in your own spiritual walk. Keep the prayers concise, the Lord knows all the details and it will help prevent an opportunity for gossip and rabbit trails to develop. This area of prayer is where many of us will grow, sometimes by leaps and bounds. This is also the purest form of fellowship! When we pray for each other revealing our deep heart issues, our crucial needs that only God can deliver, and admitting to areas where our repentance is required, we see each other with the eyes of Jesus. Recognizing those areas where you may fall short and realizing that you cannot change without the help of your Father is a huge step in getting closer to Him. Like a father holding his child's hand, God desires to guide us through the perils of life and He longs to celebrate our victories and accomplishments. As believers, our desire should be to hear from Him, "Well done".

Scripture says, *"Rejoice with those who rejoice and weep with those who weep." Romans 12:15 (ESV)* Sharing your praises and your prayer requests, is one way to live this out. Share only one praise report and one prayer request. Use the space called, "What happened?" to share how God answered the prayers. It is greatly encouraging to record this piece, as you begin to see God working in your life, hearing you and responding to your prayers. If you did not know, you will learn that you can count on God to hear and answer all of your prayers. Sometimes, the answer comes later than when you want or in a way that you did not expect, but it always comes. Other times the answer will be "no", but we need to trust that God knows what is best for us. Therefore, you may not be able to fill in the "What Happened?" section in the weeks to come, don't be discouraged. You are His child and He loves you so much. Be patient and wait on Him, He will respond. When He does, record it and praise Him!

Name	Date *8/1/2011*	Prayer & Praise	What Happened?
Jane	**Praise**	*The Lord gave me some much needed sunshine*	
	Prayer	*Lord, help me to see the areas in my life that take me away from You.*	*The Lord showed me that I am on the internet too much*
Margie	**Praise**	*Thank You Lord for loving me, even when I am being so unlovable.*	
	Prayer	*Lord, help me to be the wife I need to be for my husband.*	*I am learning to listen more to my husband's needs.*

Ready to Dig?
Supplies & Preparation Ideas

Now that you are done learning how to fill in these worksheets, it is time for you to get digging. Here are a few things you will need to get prepared to begin your study. Make sure you have plenty of pencils, highlighters, page flags, and post-it notes. Next, you will want a notebook or binder. This will help keep your research together. If possible, get dividers for your notebook. This will help you to organize your research. If you are facilitating a group, use a file box for your study group. After you download the worksheets from the internet, you will make copies and can then organize those copies in the file box. Depending on your group size, have at least fifteen to twenty-five copies of each page available for your study group. If you are doing a study on your own, you can choose to download and print the worksheets as you need them. Don't forget your resources! For your **free downloads** of these worksheets and links to some of the recommended resources, please go to **www.sowersstudy.com** and click on the "downloads" tab. Enter the password *Psal19105* and follow the directions for the download. Remember that with this expanded edition, you will have extra worksheets to download and ponder. My desire is that you will take time to reflect on the heart issues addressed in these worksheets. "All Scripture is breathed out by God and is profitable for teaching, for reproof, for correction, and for training in righteousness…" 2Timothy 3:16.

I would also strongly recommend that you familiarize yourself with the resources suggested. Knowing how to use these resources will help make your study time more focused on studying the Word. When you have completed your first study, transfer your completed worksheets to a file folder and download new worksheets. Now you can start a new study. You can use this tool over again and for any book in the Bible!

I am overjoyed that you are willing to take on this study tool. It is with great hope that you will truly that His Word is alive and that you will understand how to apply it to your life. It has been a blessing to be used by the Lord to bring you this simple tool that helps you study God's Word. It is by His Grace that this is possible, and I pray that you will also see His love and His amazing grace for you. "In the beginning the Word was with God" and by His love it is now with all of us. I pray that you will find a new zeal as you dig deep to see how to "rightly divide the Word of Truth".

In His Amazing Grace!
Margie Balcos

Made in the USA
San Bernardino, CA
04 January 2016